Life in a Tidal Pool

ALVIN and VIRGINIA SILVERSTEIN

Life in a Tidal Pool

Illustrated by

Pamela and Walter Carroll

Little, Brown and Company BOSTON · TORONTO · LONDON

First Edition

Library of Congress Cataloging-in-Publication Data

Silverstein, Alvin
    Life in a tidal pool/by Alvin and Virginia Silverstein;
illustrated by Pamela and Walter Carroll.
        p.   cm.
    Summary: Describes the varied forms of shore life found in and
around tidal pools and discusses their struggle for survival.
    ISBN 0-316-79120-2
    1. Tide pool ecology — Juvenile literature.   [1. Tide pool
ecology.   2. Ecology.]   I. Carroll, Pamela, ill.   II. Carroll,
Walter, ill.   III. Title.
QH541.5.S35S55   1990
574.5′2636 — dc20   89-12676
                                                        CIP
                                                        AC

10 9 8 7 6 5 4 3 2 1

BP

Published simultaneously in Canada
by Little, Brown & Company (Canada) Limited
Printed in the United States of America

Contents

Chapter One

At the Ocean's Edge

*M*orning *sunlight beams down on the rocky coast. Small pools of water in* rocky hollows sparkle as the sunbeams strike them. They are as still and smooth as mirrors now. Only a few shreds of seaweed, caught on the rocks like tattered rags, give a hint of the violent storm that swept over the coast the night before. Winds whipped at the waves and sent them pounding onto the rocks. The tide flooded in, higher than usual. When the storm died down and the tide went out, new pools were left among the rocks.

Beneath the quiet surface of these tidal pools, hundreds of life stories are unfolding. Ocean creatures, washed in by the waves, are settling down in their new homes. A fish darts through the water, powered by graceful sweeps of its tail. A crab with eyes on stalks like periscopes scoots along the bottom, looking for something to eat. A mussel has found a comfortable spot to settle down and is busily tying itself down to the rocks. Another mussel — less fortunate — is being eaten by a prowling starfish. Floating in the water is a swarm of life: tiny plants and animals too small to see without a microscope.

Tidal pools provide a place of shelter for the creatures at the edge of the sea. Twice each day, the tides go in and out. At high tide, the whole beach is covered with water. At low tide, large strips of land are left dry, beyond the reach of the waves. At certain times of the year, the high tides reach farther into the land; at other times, these coasts stay dry for days or weeks.

The creatures that live in the tidal zone have to be adaptable. Sometimes their homes are under water; other times they are dry. How can they survive when the tide is out? Some have hard shells that they can close tightly, keeping their own tiny sea world inside. Others may dig themselves down into the sand or mud and lie there, quiet, until the tide returns. Tidal pools provide miniature sea worlds where the coastal creatures can take refuge while the tide is out.

Not all ocean dwellers can survive in a tidal pool. Living conditions there can be very different from the sea.

Out in the ocean, the temperature of the water stays fairly even. Sunlight warms the surface waters during the day. At the bottom, where the sun's rays cannot reach, it is very cold. But in any part of the sea the temperature changes very little, and very slowly, because there is so much water there to spread out any extra warmth.

In a tidal pool, though, there is much less water. When the tide flows out, the sunlight

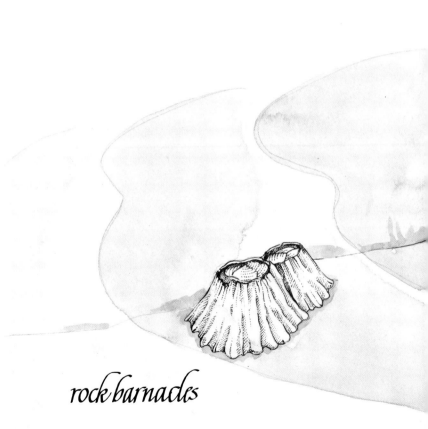

rock barnacles

quickly heats up the water in the pool. At night, the water in the tidal pool may just as quickly cool down. Only animals and plants that do not mind changes in temperature can survive there.

starfish devouring mussel

The extra heat causes other problems, too. Oxygen, a gas that both animals and plants need to breathe, is part of the air. Some of the oxygen dissolves in the water of oceans and pools. But warm water cannot hold as much oxygen as cool water. As the tidal pool heats up under the sun, it loses some of its oxygen. There may not be enough left for the pool animals to breathe.

Out in the ocean, the wind and waves whip the surface waters into a froth, and oxygen and other gases from the air are constantly being added to the water. This does not happen in the quiet tidal pool. But the plants in the pool can help — at least, during the daytime. In the sunlight, the microscopic plants and sea-weed store away energy and make food. This process is called *photosynthesis*. (The *photo* comes from a Greek word meaning "light.") Photosynthesis has an important by-product: oxygen! In fact, the oxygen we breathe is re-leased into our atmosphere by plants on land and in the ocean. Thanks to photosynthesis, the plants in the tidal pool can help replace the oxygen that leaves the water when the sunlight warms it.

Another thing warming can do is make the water in the tidal pool evaporate faster. The water turns from a liquid form into a gas and floats away into the air. The salts in the water cannot evaporate, so they stay behind. Gradually the water in the pool gets saltier. It may get too salty for some ocean creatures. They lose water from their bodies and may shrivel up and die.

When it rains, fresh water is added to the tidal pools. Then they may not be salty enough. Water floods into the bodies of the pool dwellers; they swell up and may even burst!

Only the animals and plants that can get rid of extra salt and water can thrive in the world of the tidal pool.

The waves that pound the seashore are another danger in the miniature sea worlds. Each minute, four or five waves crash against the shore. They strike with amazing force, as much as thousands of pounds of pressure on each

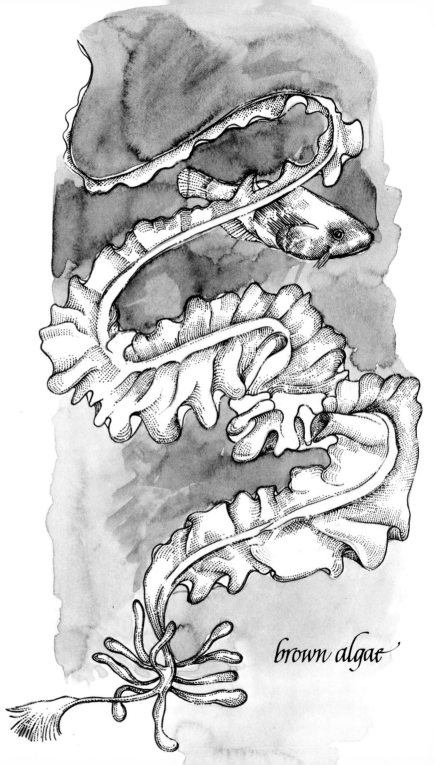

brown algae

square foot of sand or rock. When the water of each wave flows back out to sea, it pulls against the shore, sucking anything loose back with it.

Seashore creatures have developed many ways to fight the tides. Seaweeds anchor themselves to rocks with rootlike, branching holdfasts. They can cling tightly through all but the worst storms. The stalks and fronds (leaflike bodies) of these sea plants are not rigid, for then they might snap under the pull of the waves. Instead, they are limp. The seaweed fronds bend with the movement of the water, swaying back and forth. When the tide goes out, the plants collapse into a heap, protecting their precious store of moisture. When the tide comes back in, air-filled bladders help to lift the fronds and hold them upright in the water. The seaweeds provide shelter for many small animals, which cling to the fronds or hide among the holdfasts.

Some of the animals of the tidal zone can also hold on tightly against the battering of the waves. Barnacles cement themselves onto a

Irish moss

rocky surface. Water flows smoothly around their cone-shaped bodies. Mussels also tie themselves down permanently, with ropes of a plasticlike substance. Their shells are streamlined to allow the water to flow over them without dragging them away. Both the barnacles and the mussels can close their shells tightly to hold water when the tide is out.

7

Snails do not settle down for life the way barnacles and mussels do, but they can hold tight against the waves. The bottom of a snail's muscular foot grips a rock like a suction cup. A starfish clings in a similar way; instead of one big suction cup, though, it has many tiny tube feet running down its underside. Together, they can hold on with tremendous strength. The sea urchin, a relative of the starfish, looks like a pincushion, with spines sticking out all over its round body. It uses these needlelike spines to wedge itself firmly into a crack or hollow. Another relative, the sand dollar, digs itself into the sand to wait out the tide. Various clams and sea worms also spend much of their lives in sandy burrows. When the tide is in, they may come out to feed.

Life in the tidal pool, like life out in the ocean, is a constant struggle. The creatures of the pool must battle not only the waves and the weather but also one another. The variety of these life-forms and the many ways they solve their problems are endlessly amazing. Let's take a closer look at some of the interesting creatures that live in tidal pools.

snail on the move

Chapter Two

Miniature Sea Worlds

*T*idal pools are found on all the coasts of the world, wherever land and ocean meet. Each one is different — a tiny world of its own, yet also a part of the ocean that formed it. The animals and plants in a tidal pool on a rocky coast in Maine are very different from those that live in pools on the California coast or in tropical coral reefs. Yet each tidal pool is a whole community of life. In some ways this little world is very much like the larger world of the ocean.

The lives of ocean creatures are linked together in many complicated ways. These chains of life start with plants, which can use the energy of sunlight to make their own food.

Animals feed on the plants. These animals may in turn be eaten by others. The chains of life do not stop when the animals and plants die. Their bodies are broken down by bacteria and other tiny creatures and provide food for still other water dwellers.

Life in the tidal pool, as in the sea world, starts with *plankton*. That name comes from a Greek word that means "wanderer." Swarms of tiny plankton creatures, many of them too small to see without a microscope, float in the water. Some of the plants and animals in the plankton are single living cells. Your body is made up of trillions of cells, which work together to keep it functioning. But the single-

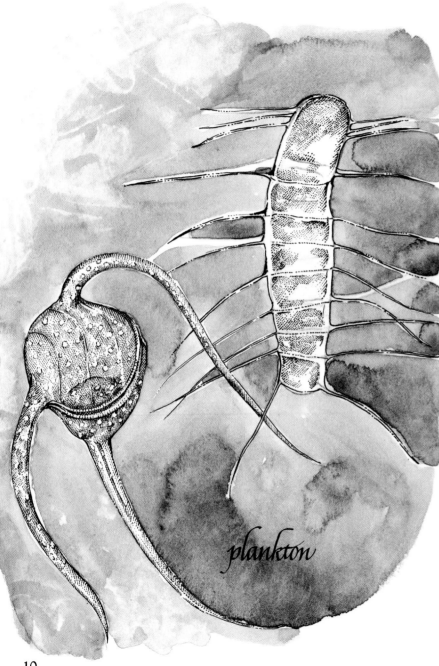

plankton

celled plankton creatures can get along on their own. Sunlight, water, and the salts and gases in the water are all they need to live.

Most plants on land are green. They contain a green chemical called *chlorophyll* that captures some of the energy from sunlight. Plants use this energy to make food out of water and carbon dioxide, a gas from the air. Ocean plants also use chlorophyll, but not all of them are green. They can be brown, golden brown, blue-green, or even red. The green of their chlorophyll is hidden by other colored chemicals that help in capturing energy.

The single-celled plants are various forms of *algae*. This group includes forms that are nothing but tiny round cells, each containing a bit of living matter, a colored chemical for trapping sunlight energy, and stored food. Some single-celled algae are joined together into chains or balls of cells. Still others are much larger and more complicated; they are more like the plants on land and may grow to be several inches or even many feet long.

The plankton algae also include the *diatoms*,

tiny single-celled creatures whose soft bodies wear a coat of armor: a shell made of hard *silica*. Sand is a form of silica, and so is glass. Under a microscope, the shells of the diatoms are beautiful, an endless variety of delicate crystal designs.

Dinoflagellates are algae with a name that means "whirling whip." Two threadlike flagella lash back and forth like tiny whips, making the dinoflagellates spin like tops in the water. Some of these algae contain a red chemical. At times, they multiply to huge numbers, turning the water blood red or brown. These "red tides" can be deadly. The dinoflagellates produce a poison that can kill fish that eat them.

Floating and swimming among the plankton are many small animals that feed on the algae. Some of them are single-celled, too. Some are larger and look like tiny shrimps or spiders. *Copepods* are tiny crustaceans, related to crabs and shrimps. Their name means "oar-foot," and they swim along in a jerky motion, with their legs working like tiny oars. Many of the

dinoflagellates

copepods are too small to see without a microscope; the largest ones grow to only half an inch long. These small animals are found among the plankton in huge numbers. They feed on diatoms, eating as much as their own weight in a day. In turn, they are eaten by fish and sea birds.

Many of the tiny plankton creatures are *larvae* — the young forms of larger animals. Often the larvae look very different from their parents. Who could guess that one active, free-swimming larva could turn into a barnacle that grows an armored shell and glues itself down onto a rock, never to move again? Another larva will grow up to be a five-armed starfish, and still another tiny creature of the plankton is the young form of a clam.

Most of the plankton animals are very small, but one big exception is the *jellyfish.* Full-grown jellyfish are usually seen in tidal pools only in the fall. A rather simple animal, shaped like a bell or an umbrella, the jellyfish has a body that is nearly 98 percent water. It looks helpless as it floats along, but it has some deadly weapons. Tentacles that can shoot out poison darts dangle from the underside of its body. If a fish or other sea creature brushes against the tentacles, the darts sting it again and again until it is paralyzed. Meanwhile, tentacles wrap around the unlucky prey and pull it up into the jellyfish's mouth, which is the only opening in the animal's body.

The jellyfish starts life at the surface as a tiny pear-shaped larva. After a while it settles to the bottom and attaches itself to a rock or a piece of seaweed. The young jellyfish, now called a *polyp* in this phase of its life, changes its shape to look like a tiny stack of saucers. It catches small sea creatures with its short tentacles and stinging darts. The polyp slowly grows through the cold winter. Then, in the spring, each little saucer breaks off, swims away, and floats on the surface as a tiny *medusa,* or free-swimming jellyfish. By the summertime, it is a full-grown adult.

The jellyfish is only one of many hunters in the tidal pool. Fish, crabs, and various other water creatures feed on the plankton animals.

medusa

jellyfish larva

ephyra

scyphistoma

polyp

In turn, they may be eaten by still other animals. In the tidal pool, as in the larger world of the ocean, the living creatures are linked into complicated food chains.

Many animals live on the microscopic plants of the plankton, but few eat the larger plants — the seaweeds. These plants play a different role in the world of the tidal pool. Floating in the water or anchored to the bottom, they provide a home and a refuge for sea animals.

Chapter Three

~~~~~~

Anchored to the Bottom

The bottom of a tidal pool is filled with life. The seaweeds that cover the rocks are as strange and varied as the plants in a tropical jungle.

Huge *kelp* trail brownish ribbons through the water or hold up broad fronds that look like rubbery leaves. One kind, with a ruffled edge, is known as "devil's apron."

Brownish-green *rockweeds* and *bladder wrack* have little air-filled bubbles scattered over their fronds. Children who find bits of these seaweeds washed up on the beach love to squeeze the air bladders and make them pop. In the living plant, they help the fronds float in the water after the tide comes in.

Sea lettuce is a green alga with thin, bright green fronds that look like lettuce leaves. Another green alga, *sea hair*, forms thin, hollow threads. Sea hair is a very hardy seaweed that can survive in the higher tidal pools. Even if the pool dries out, sea hair can live on until the next tide — as long as there is at least a little moisture from the splashing spray of the waves.

Most of the red algae are deeper-water forms, but a few hardy kinds are found in tidal pools. These include *Irish moss* and *dulse*, which some people like to eat as seaweed pudding.

Some of the "plant life" on the bottom of the pool are really animals! One kind is the

rockweed

sea lettuce

sponge, which may spread over the rocks in a thin crust or stand up like a small shrub. Most of the "sponges" sold in stores for bathing or cleaning are made of plastic, but some fine-quality bath sponges are real. They don't look as though they were ever alive. Actually, a bath sponge is just the animal's skeleton. When the sponge was alive, this skeleton was covered with soft flesh.

A sponge is not a very complicated animal; in fact, it is little more than a group of cells living and working together. Water flows in and out through the many holes and branching channels in the sponge's body. Whiplike flagella on some of the cells lining the channels keep the water moving. Other cells gobble up bits of food in the water and digest them.

Another plantlike animal on the bottom is the *sea squirt*. It looks as though it is as simple as a sponge — just a leathery bag with two spouts that pulls water in and squirts it out again. The sea squirt isn't born that way, though. Its larva looks like a tiny tadpole, and it even has a long cordlike structure down its

16

sponges

sea squirts

back very much like the backbone in higher animals. What a change the sea squirt larva goes through! It starts out as a free-swimming creature among the plankton, but then it settles down, loses its tadpole tail and its almost-backbone, and attaches itself to the bottom. There it will stay for the rest of its life, sucking in water to strain out bits of food.

Scattered among the plant life at the bottom of the pool are *sea anemones*, which look like flowers, with their delicate, beautifully colored petals waving gently in the water. These sea anemones may be beautiful, but they aren't plants — and they can be deadly! If a small fish happens to touch one of the "petals" as it swims by, suddenly the flower-creature comes to life. Dozens of poisoned darts shoot out at the fish, stinging and stunning it. Sticky threads shoot out to lasso the fish, wrapping it up securely. Dart-tipped threads continue to sting it until it is paralyzed. Then the anemone's "petals," which are really tentacles, draw its prey into a large mouth hidden in the middle of the waving tentacles. This mouth leads right

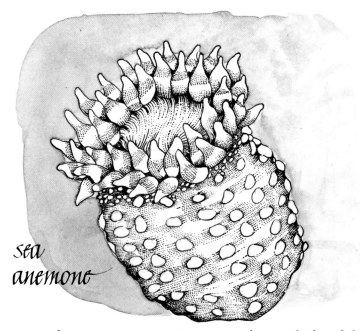

sea anemone

into the sea anemone's stomach, and the fish becomes a meal.

Does the sea anemone sound familiar, with its tentacles and stinging darts? It should, for it is a relative of the jellyfish. The jellyfish's body is like a sea anemone flattened out and turned upside down. In the jellyfish the mouth is underneath and the tentacles hang down; a sea anemone's mouth and tentacles are at the top.

Sea anemones usually spend most of their life in one spot, attached to the rocky bottom like the seaweeds. But some of them can move. They go so slowly that you would hardly notice it. First the bottom of the stalk lets go of its hold on the rock, and then it slides along, like the foot of a snail. In an hour the sea anemone travels only three or four inches. Other sea anemones just let go and float, allowing the current in the water to carry them to a new spot. Some turn cartwheels when they move. Their tentacles send them spinning end over end.

When a sea anemone moves, sharp rocks may tear its delicate body into pieces. But that doesn't harm it. In fact, each piece can grow into a perfect little sea anemone.

Some sea anemones are hitchhikers. They attach themselves to the shell of a passing crab. This can turn into a long-term partnership. The stinging tentacles of the anemone protect the crab from its enemies. Meanwhile, the anemone picks up free meals. The crab is a messy eater, tearing its prey apart. Bits of food in the water are gathered by the sea anemone's tentacles.

It's not likely that anyone would mistake a *mussel* or a *barnacle* for a plant, even though both also spend most of their lives in one spot, firmly attached to the bottom. But some people tend to get mussels and barnacles mixed up with each other. Both of these water animals are covered by hard shells, like a suit of armor protecting their soft insides. Otherwise, though, they are quite different.

Mussels are close relatives of clams. Like clams, their suit of armor is in the form of two shells, which fit together tightly. When the tide goes out, the tight seal of the shells keeps some water inside, so that the mussel's soft body will not dry out. When the pool is filled with water, the shells open, and the mussel begins to feed. It is a filter feeder. Cells on the mussel's soft body are covered by thousands of tiny, hairlike *cilia,* which beat back and forth. The movement of the cilia sets up a current in the water that carries it along the gap between the open shells. The sea water flows past

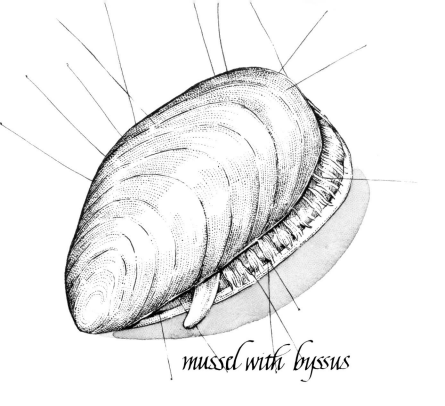

mussel with byssus

the mussel's gills, which take in oxygen, and its mouth, which filters out the tiny one-celled creatures that it eats.

Like many sea animals, the mussel starts its life as a larva among the plankton floating at the surface. Cilia help the tiny larva to swim. By the second day of its life, the mussel larva has a little yellow shell. It is a single shell at first, not the two shells connected by a hinge that adult mussels have. As the young larva grows, it loses its cilia. The weight of its growing shell would make it settle to the bottom if it were not for a bubble of air trapped inside it. This bubble keeps the larva floating at the top for a month or so, as it looks for a good place to settle down.

The young mussel is still only one-fiftieth of an inch long when it is ready to change its way of life. It settles to the bottom and moves along the rocks, gliding along with the help of cilia on its foot. If it finds a good spot, it squeezes out a thick liquid that is like a quick-setting plastic, which promptly hardens when it comes in contact with air or water and forms a clump of ropelike strands called a *byssus*. These threads tie the mussel down to the bottom.

The young mussel may change its mind and move several times as it grows. It cuts the threads and glides away, then forms new byssus threads to settle down in a new spot. Eventually, when it has grown into a three-inch adult with deep blue shells, the mussel no longer moves. Larger numbers of mussels live in the tidal pool, attached to rocks, half-buried

logs, old shells — almost anything solid.

During the mating season, a female mussel squirts millions of eggs into the water, like a milky cloud. As this stream of eggs passes, the male sends out tiny sperm that join with the eggs to form the next generation of young mussels. Only a few of the larvae grow up to become adults. Most of them are eaten by other sea creatures.

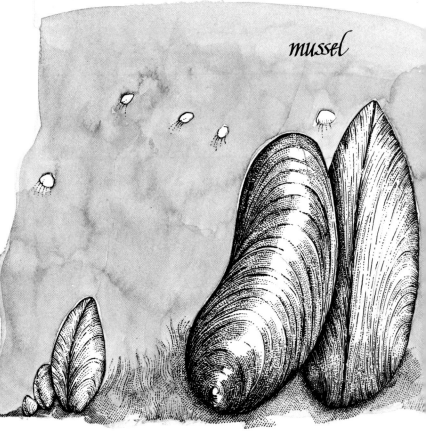

mussel

The barnacle also starts its life as a tiny swimming larva. It looks like a little water flea, and it swims among the plankton using three pairs of legs like tiny oars. A single eye helps the barnacle larva to see where it is going and to find the one-celled plant plankton on which it feeds.

After a few days, the larva sheds its skin. The old skin was hiding a surprise: the larva has changed its shape. Now it has six pairs of legs, two large feelers, and two more eyes. It looks like a little shrimp.

Now the barnacle is ready to find a place to settle down. It seems to be attracted to places where there are plenty of other barnacles. Scientists have found that barnacle larvae can recognize a special chemical that the adult barnacles produce. It probably won't settle down right on top of another barnacle, though. Usually it finds itself a bare spot.

When a mussel settles down, it goes in foot first. But a barnacle turns upside down and stands on its head. Using a very tough cement that it makes itself, it glues its head to a stone

rock barnacles

or a piece of wood. A hard, limy shell grows around the barnacle like a box. This box has a trapdoor lid. When it is open, the barnacle sticks its hairy legs out and waves them around in the water, to catch bits of food and bring them in to its mouth. If danger threatens — or if the tide goes out — the trap door closes tightly. A bit of sea water is held inside the boxy shell, and the barnacle can wait until it is safe to open up again.

An adult barnacle is a *hermaphrodite,* which means that it is both a male and a female at the same time. It mates with other barnacles nearby by sticking out a hollow tube that pokes through a gap in the other barnacle's shell. The same barnacle can be a father, by giving sperm to one of its neighbors, and also a mother, when it receives sperm to join with its own eggs. It takes about four months for the eggs to develop inside their parent's body. Even then, they are not allowed to hatch until there is plenty of food in the water.

The larva's life is a dangerous one, swimming near the surface. Many of the larvae are eaten. Only about one in a thousand survives to grow up into an adult. But that is enough to make barnacles one of the most common creatures in the tidal pool. One scientist counted nearly thirty thousand acorn barnacles, each up to three inches long, on just one square yard along the shore!

acorn barnacles

Chapter Four

On the Move

*T*he quiet waters of the tidal pool seem peaceful on the surface. Down in the underwater jungle, though, hunters stalk their prey, prowling along the bottom or swimming among the trailing seaweed fronds.

Things are not always what they seem — like that sponge, crawling along the bottom. Sponges don't crawl! It is really a crab, holding a sponge on its back with two hind feet. The crab is using the sponge for camouflage, to sneak up on the little water creatures it catches and eats. The sponge provides some protection, too. Larger water animals do not like to bite into a sponge and crunch down on the tiny bonelike spikes that form its inner skeleton.

A purple *starfish* seems to flow over the rocks as it moves. A mussel quickly snaps its shells shut when the starfish comes near. But the five-armed animal flows right over the mussel, and then a tug-of-war begins. It is a fight to the death, and it will be the mussel who loses.

On the underside of each of the starfish's five arms are rows of tiny tube feet with suction-cup ends. These tube feet are connected to a set of water pipes running through the starfish's body. By filling some of the tube feet with water and emptying others, it can move its whole body along or grip tight to a rock or a shellfish. Its pull is strong and steady, and it can keep it up for a long time. Some of the tube feet rest while the others work, and then they take over the grip.

Finally the tired mussel gets weaker. Its shells open — just a tiny bit, but that is enough for its enemy. Through the mouth at the center of its underside, the starfish turns its stomach inside out! A part of the stomach comes slithering out and slips through the gap between the mussel's shells. Powerful chemicals start to flow out of the starfish's stomach. It digests the mussel's soft body, right inside its own shell, until it is just a soupy mass. Then the starfish pulls its stomach back in and sucks up its meal. All that is left of the mussel is a pair of empty shells.

starfish with sea urchin

"Starfish" is not really a very good name for this sea animal. It is shaped like a five-pointed star, but it is not a fish. It belongs to a group of animals called *echinoderms,* which means "spiny skin." It has an inner skeleton made of limy plates. On its back it has a number of little clawlike pincers. If a barnacle tries to settle on a starfish's back, the pincers clamp onto it. Then a current produced by hairlike cilia, beating back and forth, carries the unsuccessful hitchhiker to the starfish's mouth. The pincers also come in handy as weapons if an enemy — perhaps another starfish — tries to attack. Red eyespots at the tips of the starfish's arms help it to watch for enemies and find its prey. It may curl the tips of its arms upward, looking around with its eyespots.

Bivalves — two-shelled mollusks such as clams, mussels, and oysters — are the starfish's favorite food, but it may also eat snails, sea cucumbers, and even fish and shrimps, as well as bits of dead matter on the bottom. People who gather oysters consider the starfish a terrible pest. Oystermen used to chop up the starfish they caught and throw the pieces back into the sea. But they were just making things worse, for a piece of a starfish can grow back all the missing parts to form a whole new starfish!

Starfish also have a more usual way of making new starfish. During the mating season, the female releases a cloud of tiny eggs — millions of them — into the water. A nearby male sends out a cloud of sperm, and the male and female cells join. The tiny larvae, which don't look at all like starfish, swim among the plankton. They grow and change until — as tiny, brightly colored five-pointed stars — they settle down to the bottom.

The *sea urchin,* one of the starfish's relatives, really lives up to the echinoderms' "spiny skin" name. Its ball-shaped body is covered with sharp spines, so that it looks like a pincushion with the pins all pointing outward. Each spine is attached to its inner limy shell by a movable joint. The sea urchin uses its spines, along with tube feet, to move around. The spines also help to wedge it securely into cracks when the tide is going out, and they provide some protection — who would want to bite into a pincushion?

Another relative, the *sea cucumber*, has a soft body without spines or a limy inner skeleton. Its long body looks like a cucumber, but it has a mouth surrounded by tentacles at one end. It can squeeze into cracks between rocks or hide in a burrow in the sand.

The garden slugs that live on the land are slimy creatures that most people find ugly. But their cousins the *sea slugs* are among the most beautiful animals in the undersea world. They are brightly colored, and their backs are decorated with feathery gills that help them breathe. Actually, their soft bodies are naturally colorless, but they take on the color of the food they eat.

Sea slugs seem to specialize in eating things most animals won't touch. Some feed on sponges. Others eat jellyfish and sea anemones. The stinging cells that defend these animals from other enemies do not bother sea slugs at all. They just cover the poison darts with slime

limpet

and go right on munching away, nibbling on tentacles and swallowing the stinging cells whole. These poison darts pass right through the sea slug's body unchanged and are stored away on the sea slug's back. If an enemy tries to eat a sea slug, it is zapped by these borrowed defenses. Most animals quickly learn not to bother sea slugs.

Sea slugs are relatives of snails. Like their shelled cousins, most sea slugs move along on

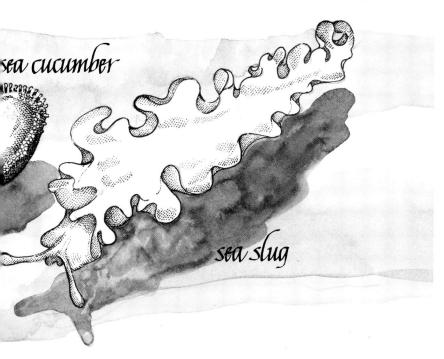

sea cucumber

sea slug

a muscular foot, prowling around the rocks and hiding in cracks when they are not feeding. A few kinds do not have a foot. Instead, they swim through the water by paddling with their gills or gracefully waving their long bodies.

The eggs of sea slugs hatch into tiny swimming larvae. Growing among the plankton, they change into tiny snaillike animals with a shell. But by the time the sea slug has grown into an adult, its shell has disappeared.

The little world of the tidal pool includes a number of real shelled snails, too. They are usually to be found crawling along the bottom or clinging to rocks.

The *limpet* is a snail with a shell that looks like a tent, or a cone. The keyhole limpet has a hole at the top of its shell, which looks like a miniature volcano. It uses this hole to get rid of its body wastes and extra water.

Most of the limpet's soft body stays protected inside its shell, but it may poke out its head and its foot. The head has two big tentacles that look like ears, each with an eye at its base. The foot is broad and muscular. It can cling to a rock with a strength that is amazing. When a limpet is holding on, you cannot easily lift it or pull it off its perch.

Each limpet has its own place on the rocks. Whenever one decides to settle down, it rubs against the rock with its shell and wears away the rock until a shallow depression is formed, exactly the right size and shape for the limpet to fit. When it goes off to feed, slithering slowly along on its muscular foot, it doesn't wander far from home — usually just two or three feet. Before the tide goes out, it heads back. Somehow it is able to find its way to its own particular spot.

Unlike its cousin the sea slug, the limpet is not a hunter. It lives on plants, scraping algae off rocks and ripping apart seaweed. It feeds with its tongue, which is kept coiled up like a watchspring when it is not being used. This tongue, called a *radula*, is lined with hard "teeth," which make it like a file.

Strangely, most limpets start their life as males. But when they become larger, perhaps an inch or two, some of them become females. After a time there are just about as many females as males. Scientists believe that adult females send out a chemical into the water that makes the young ones in the neighborhood grow into males. But some of these young males move away to find new homes and thus get away from the chemical. Then they can change into females.

Limpets breed during the cold months, sending their eggs out into the water. A tiny larva, only 1/120 of an inch long, hatches out in about twenty-four hours. Hairlike cilia help it to swim among the plankton. It does not look anything like a snail yet. In another day or so it grows a tiny shell, but still doesn't look like a snail. Eventually settling down to the bottom, it gradually changes and grows into an adult limpet.

Surprisingly, one of the commonest snails found along the Atlantic coast of the United States and Canada did not arrive on this continent until about a century and a half ago. These are the *periwinkles*, brought over to Nova Scotia around 1840 by settlers from Europe. The colonists may have brought them on purpose, to raise as food animals, or the snails may have hitched a ride on the hulls of ships. Nobody is quite sure. At any rate, these little snails have quickly settled down in their new home. On some New England coasts they cover the beaches, as many as five hundred or more in a square yard.

The periwinkle's cone-shaped shell can grow up to an inch and a half across. The shell is usually black, but sometimes brown or red, with stripes around its coils. When the tide is out, these snails cling tightly to rocks with their muscular foot or hide in crevices. A hard, round structure, called the "winkle head," attached to the periwinkle's foot, closes its mouth tightly during low tide, to keep it from drying out. (The winkle head is not the snail's real head, which has two tentacles, each with an eye at the base.)

When the tidal pool is filled with seawater, periwinkles can be seen crawling along the bottom. Their foot is rather unusual: it comes in two parts, a right and a left. Each part works after the other, so that the snail seems to walk along — at a snail's pace, of course.

Like its relative the limpet, the periwinkle feeds on algae and seaweed, scraping them off rocks with its filelike radula. This tongue is more than two inches long — longer than the periwinkle's whole body!

Periwinkles mate in the spring. Each female can lay up to five thousand eggs in a season. The eggs are laid in tiny capsules, each holding

periwinkle

one to three eggs, that float at the surface. In about a week, microscopic larvae hatch out and swim among the plankton. In about two or three months, the larvae — those that survive — have turned into tiny winkles, no bigger than a pinhead. These tiny snails settle down to the bottom.

Scientists studying periwinkles at Chesapeake Bay found that they have a big effect on the coast. Metal mesh cages were placed on the beach between the high- and low-tide lines. All of the snails were removed from the area covered by some of the cages. In less than a month, those areas were covered with green sea grass algae, six to eight inches tall. Without the periwinkles acting as miniature lawn mowers, the algae grew quickly and slowed down the flow of water so that bits of sand and mud could settle to the bottom. Mud worms, crabs, and other animals moved in. Soon the beach was turning into a marsh.

Another scientist, who studied the animals on the coast of Cape Cod Bay, found that nearly all the hermit crabs there were living in shells from periwinkles. What did the hermit crabs use before the periwinkles came to America? Nobody knows.

Hermit crabs are odd creatures. They carry a borrowed "house" along with them wherever they go. Their bodies are very soft. If they did not have the protection of a shell, they would

hermit crab

be easy prey for one of the prowling hunters of the tidal pool.

A hermit crab continues to grow, so after a while its borrowed shell gets too tight to fit. When a hermit crab finds an empty shell from a snail that has died, it inspects it carefully, rolling the shell over and running its claws over the inside and outside. It may try the shell on for size. If it fits, the crab abandons the old, outgrown shell and slips backward into its new home.

The hermit crab has four pairs of legs. The first ones are much larger than the rest. The right one is especially large and acts as a door, closing off the shell if the hermit crab wants to sleep or hide from an enemy. The left front leg has claws that tear apart the crab's food (small animals and plants) and help to carry bits of food into its mouth. The next two pairs of legs are used for walking. The last pair, much smaller than the rest, are for holding onto the borrowed shell. They clamp on tight, so that the shell doesn't wiggle or fall off when the hermit crab walks around.

The female hermit crab has special structures, called *swimmerets*, on her abdomen. After she mates, she carries her young in these swimmerets. From time to time she moves the swimmerets back and forth, bringing in fresh water and oxygen for the growing young. After a while the young hermit crabs leave their mother and look for shells of their own.

If a hermit crab meets another that seems to have a better shell, it may try to force the other out of its home. The two crabs fight until the winner walks away with the prize.

Chapter Five

Hiding Out

Hide and seek is a very serious game in the little world of the tidal pool. For the winners the prize is life — getting enough to eat and avoiding being eaten. A fish, lurking behind a rock, may swim out suddenly to catch an unwary shrimp. Or the shrimp may dive to safety in a narrow gap between the rocks, too small for the fish to follow. A good place to hide can make the difference for the hunter or the hunted.

Many of the tidal pool animals hide from danger by digging a refuge in the bottom. The *sand dollar* is one of them. It gets the first part of its name from its habit of burying itself in the sand. The "dollar" part comes from its shape: it is flat and round, and often just about the size of a silver dollar.

The sand dollar is another relative of the starfish and sea urchin. It does not have arms, like a starfish, but it does have a five-petaled flower design on its body. The sand dollar is an echinoderm, but its "spiny skin" is quite different from the sharp spines of the sea urchin. A sand dollar's spines are only about a sixteenth of an inch long. They cover it so thickly that its surface looks and feels like velvet. Short tube feet are found on both the upper and lower surfaces.

When a sand dollar wants to bury itself in the sand, it uses the movement of its spines to

buried and unburied sand dollars

shove one edge under at an angle. As it continues to push downward, sand piles up in front and covers it. Some sand dollars bury themselves completely, so that only their outline shows on the surface of the sand. Others leave the rear edge uncovered. Sometimes the sand dollar stands straight up on edge in the water.

Sand dollars feed on tiny water creatures and bits of food matter that have fallen to the bottom. Cilia beating on the spines set up currents in the water that draw these bits of food in until they are caught in slime that forms on the spines. The slime flows down into channels that lead along the surface of the sand dollar's body to its mouth, on the underside of its body. Five hard teeth fit together to scrape and tear the food. Chewing wears down these teeth, but they continue to grow as long as the sand dollar lives.

With its round body, you might think it would not matter to a sand dollar which way it goes when it moves. It doesn't matter to a starfish: any one of its five arms can lead the way. But a sand dollar seems to have a very

definite front edge and rear edge, and it can only move forward. If it comes up against a big rock or some other barrier, it stops, turns itself around by movements of its spines, and then heads off in a new direction, with its front edge still leading the way.

Like starfish, the sand dollar has little claw-like pincers on its upper surface. These keep animals such as barnacles from settling down on it, but they do not give much protection from such undersea hunters as snails, which can scrape a hole right through the sand dollar's hard inner skeleton with their filelike radulas. Starfish kill and eat sand dollars, too. When a starfish is coming, all the sand dollars in its path hurry to bury themselves in the sand. Of course, a sand dollar cannot hurry very well — it takes as long as three minutes to bury itself. Fortunately, starfish do not move very quickly, either.

Clams are another group of sea animals that hide from prowling starfish by burying themselves in the sand. Like mussels, clams are bivalve mollusks, whose soft bodies are covered by two limy shells, attached by a tough hinge. When an enemy is coming near, the clam pushes the tip of its foot down into the sand or mud. The tip spreads out to form an anchor, and muscles in the foot pull the rest of the clam down after it. For an animal that spends much of its time in the sand, a clam can move quickly — a razor clam, with a shell six inches long, can bury itself completely in less than seven seconds!

At the edge of the sea, where many clams live, each wave uncovers some and sends them tumbling. As soon as the wave passes, they quickly dig in again. Safe in the sand, the clam sends up a small tube like a periscope. This is the *siphon*. It sucks in seawater, along with any bits of food and microscopic plankton it contains. All this passes down the siphon into the clam's body. First the water flows over the gills, which pick up oxygen from the water. Tiny

clam

cilia on the gills set up a current that draws water into the siphon and sends it flowing along to the clam's mouth. Along the way, bits of sand, wood, and other unwanted things are separated out. The clam spits them out into the water through a separate siphon, which also sends its body wastes out into the water.

Clams come in many shapes and sizes. The tiny *coquina* clams of the Atlantic coast, whose bean-shaped shells are pink, yellow, blue, white, or purplish, may be full grown at half an inch. The giant clams of the tropical oceans, by contrast, can grow to three feet across.

The clam's powerful muscles hold its two shells together so tightly that only the pull of a starfish can part them. But other enemies have different ways around the clam's defenses. The drumfish's strong jaws can crush clamshells. A seagull flies up with a clam and drops it down onto a rock to smash it, then feasts on the soft meat inside the broken shells. Some snails can bore a hole right through the shell and eat the meat inside.

The beginning of the clam's life is even more dangerous. It starts out as a tiny swimming larva among the plankton, where it grows and changes until it is ready to settle down. The defenseless larva is easy prey for many kinds of predator. Yet somehow, huge numbers of clams manage to survive. Along one California beach four miles long, clam diggers dug up three million clams in two months — and there were still more left.

In a study of another tide pool animal, scientists took samples and figured out there must be close to 160 million worms of just one particular kind living in the sand of a strip of California beach one mile long, ten feet wide, and one foot deep.

Worms that live on land are often drab little creatures, but some of the worms of the sea are amazingly beautiful. *Peacock worms* belong to the group of *fanworms*. Most of the fanworm's body stays hidden inside a tube built from sand or bits of shell glued together by slimy mucus, or even from a parchmentlike material produced entirely by the worm. After it finishes building its tube, the fanworm stays there for life. It feeds by poking its head, with a crown of feathery tentacles, out of the tube. Cilia on the tentacles set up a current in the water that sends tiny particles down into the worm's mouth. On the way they are sorted into small bits that may be good for food, medium-sized particles that may make good building materials, and large particles that are thrown away.

At the slightest hint of danger — a passing shadow or a vibration in the water — the worm's fan-shaped head pops back into its tube. Quick as it is, sometimes a fish is even quicker and bites the head off. But that doesn't kill the worm: it can grow a new head to replace it.

Blood-red worms called *tubifex worms* crawl and burrow in the mud. They can survive in very poor conditions, such as a tidal pool that has lost most of its oxygen and become very salty. These worms live head downward in the mud, eating bits of decayed matter in it. Most of its body is inside a tube of mud and mucus that sticks up from the bottom like a chimney;

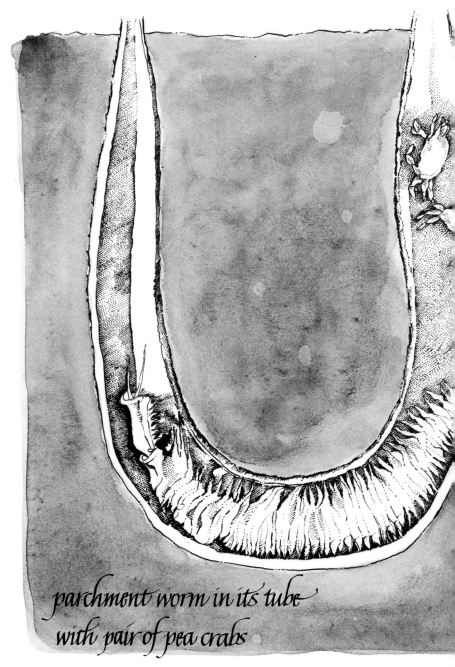

parchment worm in its tube
with pair of pea crabs

the tail end sticks out into the water. It squirms around, stirring up the water and sending new supplies of oxygen down the tube. If the amount of oxygen in the water drops, the worm backs partway out of its tube. Eventually it may come all the way out. But at the slightest sign of danger it pops back in. Sometimes a group of tubifex worms tangle up together. Their waving tails look like the tentacles of a sea anemone and help to scare away fish that might eat them.

Except for a brief time as a swimming larva, the *parchment worm* spends its whole life inside a **U**-shaped burrow in the sand. Its burrow is often shared by small *pea crabs.* The young crabs follow the stream of food-filled water that the worm keeps flowing through the tube. But if they stay for a while, they soon find that they can't leave — they have grown too big to get out of the narrow openings!

Other pea crabs live in the burrows of ghost shrimps, whose guests may also include scaleworms, smaller shrimps, and clams. They share the food and shelter there.

The various kinds of *shrimps* range in size from microscopic up to eight inches long. If you look for them in a tidal pool, you will find them hard to spot. They hide in the mud or sand at the bottom during the day and come out to feed at night. Even when they are out, their color matches the sandy bottom.

A shrimp has nineteen pairs of "legs." They aren't the kind of legs that are used for walking. Each is shaped for a special job.

The first four, two on each side, are the shrimp's feelers. It uses them to smell or taste the water, to tell it when food is near. The shrimp's eyes are on thin stalks and can move in different directions at the same time. That sounds confusing, but it is good for watching out for enemies.

The shrimp doesn't have any teeth, but it makes up for this with six pairs of "mouthparts," which grind and chew its food. Then, on the middle part of the shrimp's body, there are three pairs of "legs" with claws at the ends, which catch the shrimp's food and carry it to the mouth. Five pairs of fan-shaped swimmerets are used in swimming. And at the end a pair of "legs" forms the shrimp's tail.

The shrimp can use its tail to swim backward. Also, by using the strong muscles in its abdomen, it can race through the water at amazing speeds to escape from an enemy. Sometimes it even leaps out of the water.

Shrimps feed on small water plants and animals, as well as fish eggs and bits of leftovers from a crab's dinner. Sometimes a shrimp may even try to eat a ragworm bigger than itself.

To mate, shrimps travel out to sea as far as one hundred miles from shore. The tiny larvae look like little pears with legs. After they grow and shed their skin a few times they look like mites. Then, after two to four weeks, they look like small copies of their parents. Now they are ready to start the long and dangerous journey to the shore. Fish and other sea creatures snap them up along the way. Only about one in five may ever make it to the tidal pool. But their mother laid as many as a million eggs, so one out of five is still a lot of shrimps.

Irish moss

shrimp

Some kinds of fish get along well with shrimps. On the California coast, a little blind fish called a *goby* lives inside the burrow of the ghost shrimp. Other kinds of gobies are not blind, but in fact have very good eyesight. Many of them share the burrows of other animals. One California goby that lives with the pea crab carries in pieces of food too big to swallow. The crab tears up the food, and the goby eats the leftovers.

The frilled goby, which lives in tidal pools on the Atlantic coast, seems to have an amazing sense of direction. When the tide is out it leaps from one pool to another without even stopping to look. Yet it never winds up stranded on the beach. Skin-diving scientists who have watched this little fish very carefully have found that when it swims over the beach at high tide, it learns the layout of the bottom. It somehow seems to know that the deep spots will be water-filled pools when the tide goes out, and it remembers exactly where each one is.

Two fins on the goby's belly are shaped into a sucker that helps it cling to rocks or plants on the bottom. It is not a very good swimmer. Beats of its tail and pectoral fins send it moving through the water in jerks.

The goby is a very good parent, though. After mating, the mother lays up to a hundred eggs on the inside of an empty shell or some other solid surface. Then the father takes over, guarding the eggs until they hatch and chasing away shrimps or small fish that might eat them. After they hatch, the young gobies remain with their parents for another few weeks.

Another fish that lurks in the bottom of tidal pools, darting in and out among the rocks, is called the *grunt,* or porkfish. Despite its ugly names, it is a rather pretty fish, with bright yellow fins, two dark bands that start at its forehead, and blue and yellow stripes spreading back toward its tail.

The grunt gets its name from the sound it makes. We often think of the sea as a quiet world, but actually it is rather noisy. An underwater microphone that amplifies sounds can pick up all sorts of clicks, squeaks, and grunting noises. But the grunt makes a sound that can be heard without any artificial help. The grunting noise is made partly by the scraping of teeth located in the fish's throat. The noise is magnified by an air bladder that the grunt uses to help it rise or fall or float in the water. The air inside the bladder acts like the air inside a drum.

Like many creatures of the tidal pool, the grunt rests during the daytime and is active at night, especially just as the sun is setting or rising. That is when there is more food around — shrimps, small fish, and other small sea animals, each with a part to play in a hide-and-seek game for survival.

grunt

goby

Chapter Six

Part-Timers

Most of the creatures of a tidal pool are true water dwellers and would die if they were taken out on dry land. The pools also have some part-time dwellers, though — animals that spend only part of their lives in the water or just come down to feed.

The *ghost crab,* for example, is actually a sea animal that spends most of its life on land. It cannot breathe air; it breathes through gills that take up oxygen dissolved in seawater. Yet it digs its burrow above the high-tide line, and spends most of its active time hunting on the beach. How can it survive? It does so by carrying a supply of seawater along with it, in special gill chambers inside its body. Several times each night it goes down to a tidal pool to get a new supply of water. Sometimes, if it is frightened, it may dash into the water, but it does not swim. It just walks along the bottom until it is out on land again.

ghost crab peering out of sand

The ghost crab gets its name from its pale whitish or sand color — perfect for blending into the beach and making it hard to spot. It has eight legs for walking, running, and digging, and two claws in front for catching its prey. Its head and body are joined together, with a hard shell covering them. This shell is only about two inches across, but the crab's legs spread out widely, spanning eight inches or more. The ghost crab's two eyes are perched at the top of long stalks, so it can get a good look around, even when it is lying buried under the sand with just its eye-stalks sticking out.

The ghost crab, like other true crabs, normally walks sideways. When it has to, though, it can scuttle about quickly, frontward, backward, or in any other direction. And can it run! It is the fastest mover of all the crabs.

Ghost crabs feed mainly on *sand hoppers*, small shrimplike animals that act as a nighttime cleanup crew on the beach. Sand hoppers sleep the day away in snug burrows in the sand just above the high-tide line and come out at night to feed on bits of seaweed and dead animals that the waves have washed in. They need the dampness and salt of the seawater, so they stay near the edge of the tidal pools. But they cannot swim very well; they are much better at leaping, just like little fleas. In fact, they are sometimes called beach fleas.

The ghost crab hunts at night, when the beach fleas are out feeding. It spends the day in a burrow it has dug itself. This burrow is in the shape of a **U** or a **V**, with a main entrance and an escape hole, which is usually somewhere farther up the beach. If an enemy, such as a larger crab or a dog, digs into the main

ghost crab

entrance of the ghost crab's burrow, it can run quickly out the back door. At the bottom of the tunnel there is an enlarged den, where the crab spends the day resting.

The main entrance of the burrow stays open during the night, while the ghost crab is out hunting. The early morning hours, after it returns, are a busy time. The high tides can cause a lot of damage, and often the burrow needs to be repaired. Or the crab may dig a new one, removing the sand with its hind legs and throwing it out, far from the entrance.

The female ghost crab carries her eggs on the underside of her body. From time to time she scoops up water and sprays it on the developing babies. When they are ready to hatch, she goes down to the sea and frees the tiny larvae, which swim off and join the other creatures of the plankton. The tiny crabs molt, shedding their skin, a number of times. Each time they grow larger and change a bit. Finally the young ghost crabs crawl back to the beach and dig tiny holes in the sand. One final molt changes them into a small image of their parents. As they get larger, they slowly move up the beach, digging their burrows farther and farther from the water. But every now and then the tide washes over them.

By the time they are half grown, the young ghost crabs are living above the high-tide line. Still they continue to move up the beach, although they must return to the water to fill their gill chambers. When the October frosts come, they dig deep winter homes and shut themselves up inside. There they will sleep away the cold time and not come out until April.

Shore flies swarm around the tidal pools. These small, dark flies buzz overhead in such large numbers that they look like dark clouds. They land on the surface of the water and feed on dead insects floating there. Shore flies can actually walk on water. Their bodies are very light, and they step carefully on the surface so that they won't sink.

Another kind of shore fly lives in California and is always found where there are oil slicks. They feed on insects that have been trapped in the sticky oil, sucking their bodies dry. These shore flies lay their eggs in the ocean, where the larvae develop. The larvae are fierce and kill many tiny animals on the sea surface. Eventually they turn into adults and fly off.

Small, dark-colored insects with white or yellow markings may also be found in tidal pools. These are *shore bugs*. They kill and eat other insects. They are not very good at flying. After a short flight, they hide among rocks or under seaweed. Shore bugs have large eyes that help them to spot their next meal. They can also spot enemies approaching. If you tried to catch a shore bug, it would take off immediately as soon as you got near. For a little while it would hide somewhere near the water's edge. But soon it would be back, looking for something else to eat.

beach flea

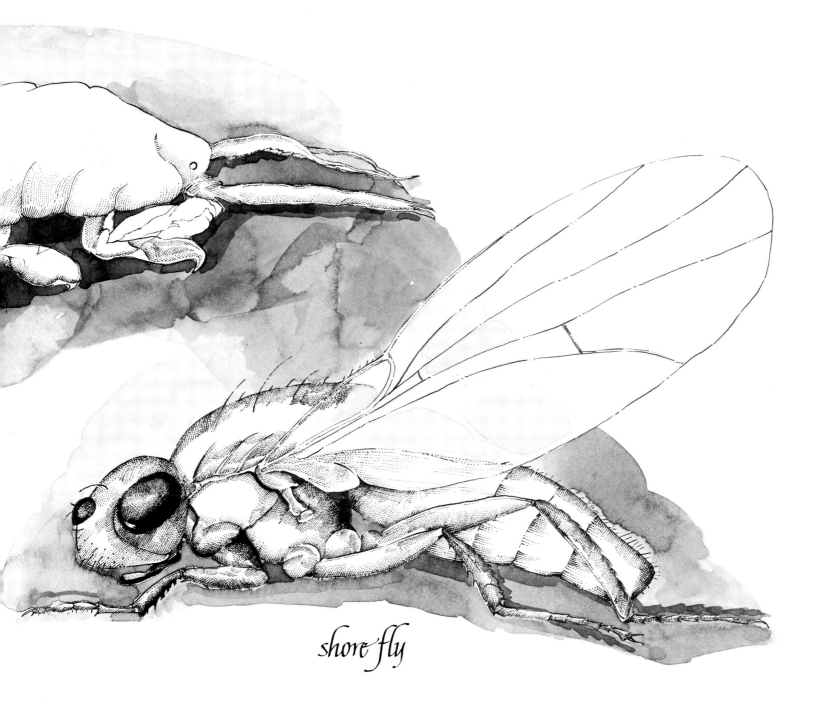

shore fly

Springtails are very common insects. Most kinds live in the soil, and they jump by flicking their tails in a sort of spring action, which gives them their name. There are some springtails living in tidal pools, too, but these have lost their ability to leap.

The bluish gray springtails are as small as gnats. They can float or even walk along the surface of the tidal pool. They carry their own "water wings" with them: a shining blanket of tiny air bubbles, trapped by hairs on the insect's body. The springtail can run along the surface of the water when it is quiet, but a ripple can set it floating helplessly. Often hundreds of these tiny insects drift together on the surface of the pool.

A springtail's biting mouth is perfect for tearing apart and eating dead matter decaying in the tidal pool. It will eat almost any dead animal: fish, mollusks, or barnacles, or bits of crab. It does much of its eating while the tide is out and the shore is exposed. When the tide comes in, it hides in crevices among the rocks, wrapped in its air blanket. It is an air-breathing animal, but it is tied to the sea; it needs the water to keep its thin, soft skin moist.

springtail

Chapter Seven

Look but Don't Touch

*S*omeday *we may travel to other planets and discover strange new forms of life. Yet there* are still plenty of exciting discoveries to be made right here on planet Earth. The world of the ocean, for example, has its share of monsters and marvels weird enough for any science fiction story. New sea creatures are discovered each year. Learning how they live, how they get along with each other, and how they solve the problems of their water world can be endlessly fascinating.

Not many people can go exploring in the ocean. Diving is an expensive and dangerous sport. But tidal pools provide a sampling of the ocean and its creatures that anyone can watch and study.

If you visit a tidal pool in the daytime, you won't see much at first. The creatures that are active during the day have good eyesight and are always on the lookout for enemies. Even your shadow could alert them. By the time you reach the edge of the pool, everything that can swim or crawl will have dived for shelter.

Be patient. Lie down at the edge of the pool and wait very quietly. Perhaps a crab will scuttle over the rocks. A fish may peep out cautiously from the seaweed jungle and then swish through the water. As you watch, the whole pool may come to life.

If you really want to learn about life in the tidal pool, you should visit it at night as well as in the daytime. Many of the creatures of the pool and the beach are asleep in some snug shelter during the daylight hours and come out only when it is dark.

Take a good flashlight along — one that can work underwater. As you walk down the beach, your beam of light may suddenly catch a ghost crab out hunting. It would normally be racing along too fast for you to get a good look. But in the beam of light it will "freeze," staying motionless and trying to blend into the sandy background. If you keep the beam on it and move slowly, being careful not to put your

hand in front of the light, it may stay still until you are quite close.

The glow of the flashlight shining underwater reveals a nighttime wonderland. The sea anemones are in full "bloom," with their petal-like tentacles waving. Sea cucumbers are poking out from the crevices where they hide during the day. Sea slugs and snails are prowling along the bottom. Swimming fish are attracted by the light and stop for a moment as they enter its beam. Shrimps with glowing red eyes swim into the beam and stare at the light. If you startle them by a sudden movement, they will leap out of the water with a splash.

It may be tempting to take some of these fascinating sea and shore creatures home with you. But unless you have a large and carefully kept saltwater aquarium, they will probably quickly die.

In some coastal areas, especially in southern California, many tidal pool creatures have been threatened by well-meaning people, eager to observe and collect them. Teachers used to take their classes on field trips to the shore at low tide. But then biologists discovered that many of the little sea communities were being wiped out. Tidal pool creatures were scooped up and carried off in buckets and bottles. Burrows were crushed. A single footstep on the soft sand or wet rocks might kill hundreds of tiny creatures.

In the world of nature, oversupply is the general rule. Sea animals lay eggs by the hundreds, thousands, or even millions. Only a few make it to adulthood, and the rest go to feed the hungry populations of hunting animals. How many creatures of a particular kind must survive for their species to continue? We don't know. So it's best to be careful as we observe these fragile, miniature sea worlds and try not to disturb the creatures that live in them.

Glossary

algae: plant forms consisting of single cells or groups of cells, from tiny diatoms to huge kelp.

barnacle: a crustacean whose adult form settles down permanently in a boxlike limy shell.

beach flea: another name for the *sand hopper.*

bivalve: a mollusk with two shells, connected by a hinge.

bladder wrack: a form of seaweed with air-filled bladders on its fronds.

byssus: a tuft of ropelike strands by which mussels anchor themselves to a solid surface.

chlorophyll: a green chemical used by plants to capture sunlight energy.

cilia: tiny hairlike structures on the surface of a cell that wave back and forth to produce movement or set up currents in the water.

clam: a bivalve mollusk that moves with a muscular foot and filters food from the water.

copepods: plankton animals that feed on diatoms and provide food for larger sea animals.

coquina: a tiny bean-shaped clam.

crustacean: a group of animals including crabs, shrimps, lobsters, and barnacles, with hard, external skeletons and many specialized "legs" (appendages).

diatoms: single-celled plankton algae covered with silica shells.

dinoflagellates: algae with whiplike flagella;

sometimes they multiply to form poisonous "red tides."

dulse: a form of red seaweed.

echinoderms: a group of "spiny skin" animals including starfish, sea urchins, and sand dollars.

fanworms: sea worms with feathery tentacles on their heads.

ghost crab: a pale-colored crab that lives on the beach but can't breathe air; it carries its own supply of sea water.

goby: a small fish that lives in burrows or crevices and comes out to feed; the father cares for the eggs until they hatch.

grunt: a striped fish that makes a grunting noise; also called the *porkfish.*

hermaphrodite: an animal with both male and female sex organs.

hermit crab: a crab that covers its soft body with an empty snail shell.

Irish moss: a form of red alga. The dried plant is used as a thickening agent in foods.

jellyfish: a soft-bodied floating animal with an umbrella-shaped body and dangling tentacles with stinging poison darts.

kelp: a large brown alga; a form of seaweed.

larva: an immature form of an animal that may look very different from the adult.

limpet: a snail with a tent-shaped shell that can cling tightly to rocks.

medusa: a name for the jellyfish in the free-swimming phase of its life.

mussel: a bivalve mollusk that filters food out of seawater.

parchment worm: a sea worm that lives inside a U-shaped burrow in the sand.

peacock worm: a sea worm that lives inside a tube and has feathery tentacles on its head.

pea crab: a sea crab that lives in a burrow, often with sea worms and small fish such as the goby.

periwinkle: a common snail with a cone-shaped shell that was brought to America from Europe.

photosynthesis: a process by which plants convert carbon dioxide and water to sugars, using energy from sunlight and producing oxygen.

plankton: small plants and animals that float in the surface waters; include algae, copepods, and various larvae.

polyp: a name for the jellyfish during the time it is attached to the sea bottom.

radula: the filelike tongue of a snail, used in feeding on plants.

rockweed: a brown alga; a seaweed with air-filled bladders on its fronds.

sand dollar: a round, flat echinoderm with short, velvety spines; it burrows into the sand.

sand hopper: a shrimplike animal that hops like a flea; a scavenger that feeds on dead matter on the beach.

sea anemone: a flowerlike animal related to the jellyfish.

sea cucumber: a cucumber-shaped echinoderm.

sea hair: a green alga that grows in thin, hollow threads.

sea lettuce: a green alga with leafy fronds.

sea slug: a brightly colored mollusk; like a snail without a shell.

sea squirt: a bag-shaped animal that has a tadpolelike larva.

sea urchin: a ball-shaped echinoderm that is covered with spines.

shore bug: a small, dark insect that can fly only a short distance.

shore fly: a small, dark fly that can land and walk on the surface of the water.

shrimp: a crustacean with nineteen pairs of "legs" (appendages), including feelers, mouthparts, claws, swimmerets, and a tail.

siphon: a tubelike structure through which a clam sucks in water.

silica: the mineral that forms sand, glass, and shells of diatoms.

sponge: a simple animal with many branching channels in its body.

springtail: an insect that floats or runs on the surface of the tidal pool and hides in crevices, wrapped in an air bubble, when the tide is in.

starfish: a star-shaped echinoderm that moves by means of tube feet on the underside of its five-armed body.

swimmerets: leglike structures under the abdomen of some crustaceans such as hermit crabs and shrimps; used for swimming or carrying eggs.

tubifex worm: a blood-red worm that can survive in salty, oxygen-poor tidal pools.